God's Little Instruction Book on Success

Tulsa, Oklahoma

God's Little Instruction Book on Success
ISBN 1-56292-084-7
Copyright © 1996 by Honor Books, Inc.
P. O. Box 55388
Tulsa, Oklahoma 74155

6th Printing

Manuscript prepared by W. B. Freeman Concepts, Inc., Tulsa, Oklahoma

Introduction

Many people would define success as fame, fortune, or a good reputation. Some may even extend the definition to include integrity of character and acts of giving. However, the achievement of all these qualities can still leave one with a sense of emptiness.

The Bible's description of a successful person is someone who has established an intimate relationship with the Heavenly Father, desiring to please Him in all areas of their life. Such a life of faith in God brings forth these qualities of success: a deep sense of fulfillment, lasting joy, and inner peace.

In the words of an anonymous writer, "Success is an *inside* story" — one that begins in the heart and radiates outwardly.

To Laugh Much And Often;
To Win the Respect Of Intelligent People
And The Affection Of Little Children;
To Earn The Appreciation Of Honest Critics
And Endure the Betrayal Of False Friends;
To Appreciate Beauty, To Find The Best In Others;
To Leave The World A Bit Better,
Whether By a Healthy Child, A Garden Patch
Or a Redeemed Social Condition;
To Know Even One Life Has Breathed Easier
Because You Lived.
This Is to Have Succeeded.

— Ralph Waldo Emerson

Blessed (happy, fortunate, prosperous, and enviable) is the man who walks and lives not in the counsel of the ungodly [following their advice, their plans and purposes]...But his delight and desire are in the law of the Lord, and on His law (the precepts, the instructions, the teachings of God) he habitually meditates (ponders and studies) by day and by night....and everything he does shall prosper [and come to maturity].

Psalm 1:1-3 AMP

And whatever we ask we receive from Him, because we keep His command- ments and do those things that are pleasing in His sight.
1 John 3:22 NKJV

~

Success in the world means power, influence, money, prestige. But in the Christian world, it means pleasing God.

Success isn't measured by the position you reach in life; it's measured by the obstacles you overcome.

Blessed is the man who perseveres under trial, because when he has stood the test, he will receive the crown of life that God has promised to those who love him.
James 1:12

I know that I have not yet reached that goal, but there is one thing I always do ...I keep trying to reach the goal and get the prize for which God called me through Christ to the life above.
Philippians 3:13-14
NCV
~

Effort is supreme joy. Success is not a goal, but a means to aim still higher.

S uccess is 10 percent inspiration and 90 percent perspiration.

The plans of the dilegent lead to profit as surely as haste leads to poverty.
Proverbs 21:5

*You need
endurance,
so that when
you have done the
will of God, you
may receive what
was promised.
Hebrews 10:36
NRSV*

We can do anything we want to do if we stick to it long enough.

A diamond is a piece of coal that stuck to its job.

When he has tested me, I shall come out like gold. My foot has held fast to his steps.
Job 23:10-11
NRSV

11

A man's pride will bring him low, but the humble in spirit will retain honor.
Proverbs 29:23
NKJV

Failure isn't so bad if it doesn't attack the heart. Success is all right if it doesn't go to the head.

He who would climb the ladder must begin at the bottom.

Anyone wanting to be a leader among you must be your servant. And if you want to be right at the top, you must serve like a slave.
Matthew 20:26-27 TLB

~

Precept upon precept, rule upon rule,...here a little, there a little...the Lord will teach.
Isaiah 28:10-11
AMP

Step by step, little by little, bit by bit — that is the way to wealth, that is the way to wisdom, that is the way to glory.

14

How can they say my life is not a success? Have I not for more than sixty years got enough to eat and escaped being eaten?

For we brought nothing into this world, and it is certain we can carry nothing out. And having food and raiment let us be therewith content.
1 Timothy 6:7-8
KJV

Lazy hands make a man poor, but diligent hands bring wealth.
Proverbs 10:4

The dictionary is the only place that success comes before work. Hard work is the price we must pay for success.

Have a purpose in life, and having it, throw into your work such strength of mind and muscle as God has given you.

Live purposefully and worthily and accurately, not as the unwise and witless, but as wise (sensible, intelligent people), making the very most of the time [buying up each opportunity].
Ephesians 5:15-16
AMP

Talk no more so very proudly, let not arrogance come from your mouth; for the Lord is a God of knowledge, and by him actions are weighed.
1 Samuel 2:3
NRSV

When success turns a man's head, he faces failure.

The first step on the way to victory is to recognize the enemy.

Discipline yourselves, keep alert. Like a roaring lion your adversary the devil prowls around, looking for someone to devour. Resist him, steadfast in your faith.
1 Peter 5:8-9
NRSV

19

Glory and honor and peace to every man who does good.
Romans 2:10
NASB

~

Everybody finds out, sooner or later, that all success worth having is founded on Christian rules of conduct.

By success, of course, I do not mean that you may become rich, famous, or powerful...I mean the development of mature and constructive personality.

Perseverance must finish its work so that you may be mature and complete, not lacking anything.
James 1:4

Then you will have success if you are careful to observe the decrees and laws that the Lord gave Moses for Israel. Be strong and courageous. Do not be afraid or discouraged.
1 Chronicles 22:13
≈

Success depends on backbone, not wishbone.

Half the failures in life arise from pulling in one's horse as he is leaping.

Jesus replied, "No one who puts his hand to the plow and looks back is fit for service in the kingdom of God."
Luke 9:62

23

Let us not get tired of doing what is right, for after a while we will reap a harvest of blessing if we don't get discouraged and give up.
Galatians 6:9 TLB

~

Success in life is a matter not so much of talent or opportunity as of concentration and perseverance.

24

There is a close correlation between getting up in the morning and getting up in the world.

A little sleep, a little slumber, a little folding of the hands to rest — and poverty will come on you like a bandit and scarcity like an armed man.
Proverbs 6:10,11

*Let the wise
also hear and
gain in learning.*
Proverbs 1:5 NRSV

I make progress by having people around me who are smarter than I am — and listening to them.

Success is being able to come home, lay your head on the pillow and sleep in peace.

His peace will keep your thoughts and your hearts quiet and at rest as you trust in Christ Jesus.
Philippians 4:7
TLB

Be careful so you will not fall from your strong faith. But grow in the grace and knowledge of our Lord and Savior Jesus Christ.
2 Peter 3:17-18
NCV
~

You've got to continue to grow, or you're just like last night's cornbread — stale and dry.

28

I t's not enough to get all the breaks. You've got to know how to use them.

He who gathers crops in summer is a wise son, but he who sleeps during harvest is a disgraceful son.
Proverbs 10:5

He is a rewarder of those who diligently seek Him.
Hebrews 11:6
NKJV

~

Success that is easy is cheap.

A purpose is the eternal condition of success.

Where there is no vision, the people perish.
Proverbs 29:18
KJV

But they all alike began to make excuses.... I tell you, not one of those men who were invited will get a taste of my banquet.
Luke 14:18,24

Ninety-nine percent of failures come from people who have the habit of making excuses.

There is in this world no such force as the force of a man determined to rise.

Let us lay aside every weight, and the sin which so easily ensnares us, and let us run with endurance the race that is set before us.
Hebrews 12:1
NKJV

Therefore, as God's chosen, set apart and enjoying His love, clothe yourselves with tenderness of heart, kindliness, humility, gentleness, patient endurance.
Colossians 3:12
MLB

To have grown wise and kind is real success.

34

T hree qualities vital to success: toil, solitude, prayer.

Do not let this Book of the Law depart from your mouth; meditate on it day and night, so that you may be careful to do everything written in it. Then you will be prosperous and successful.
Joshua 1:8

35

There is an appointed time for everything. And there is a time for every event under heaven.
Ecclesiastes 3:1
NASB

There is not a man that has not "his hour," and there is not a thing that has not its place.

Success is more a function of consistent common sense than it is of genius.

Commit your work to the Lord, then it will succeed.
Proverbs 16:3 TLB

37

Godly sorrow brings repentance that leads to salvation and leaves no regret.
2 Corinthians 7:10

≈

When you make a mistake, admit it; learn from it and don't repeat it.

Success won at the cost of self-respect is not success.

For what will a man be profited, if he gains the whole world, and forfeits his soul?
Matthew 16:26
NASB

39

Study to show thyself approved unto God, a workman that needeth not to be ashamed, rightly dividing the word of truth.
2 Timothy 2:15
KJV
~

One important key to success is self-confidence. An important key to self-confidence is preparation.

S ix essential qualities that are the key to success: sincerity, personal integrity, humility, courtesy, wisdom, charity.

Do your best to improve your faith. You can do this by adding goodness, under-standing, self-control, patience, devotion to God, concern for others, and love.... If you keep on doing this, you won't stumble and fall.
2 Peter 1:5-7,10
CEV

The people blessed all the men who willingly offered themselves.
Nehemiah 11:2
NKJV

The simple virtues of willingness, readiness, alertness, and courtesy will carry a young man farther than mere smartness.

In my vocabulary, there is no such word as "can't," because I recognize that my abilities are given to me by God to do what needs to be done.

I can do everything God asks me to with the help of Christ who gives me the strength and power.
Philippians 4:13
TLB

43

In all the work you are doing, work the best you can. Work as if you were doing it for the Lord, not for people.
Colossians 3:23
NCV

~

The man who works for the gold in the job rather than for the money in the pay envelope is the fellow who gets on.

The man who will use his skill and constructive imagination to see how much he can give for a dollar, instead of how little he can give for a dollar, is bound to succeed.

By your standard of measure, it shall be measured to you.
Matthew 7:2
NASB

Do what is right and good in the sight of the Lord.
Deuteronomy 6:18 NKJV

~

The smile of God is victory.

'Tis man's to fight,
but Heaven's
to give success.

The Lord says,
"Don't be afraid!
Don't be
paralyzed by this
mighty army! For
the battle is not
yours, but God's!"
2 Chronicles
20:15 TLB

Behold, you desire truth in the inward parts, and in the hidden part You will make me to know wisdom.
Psalm 51:6 NKJV

To be a winner in life, we must first be a winner inside.

It is sheer waste of time... to imagine what I would do if things were different. They are not different.

Brothers, I do not consider myself yet to have taken hold of it. But one thing I do: Forgetting what is behind and straining toward what is ahead.
Philippians 3:13

49

Choose for yourselves this day whom you will serve.
Joshua 24:15
NKJV

The surest way not to fail is to determine to succeed.

The only thing that stops you is yourself. Period.

Create in me a pure heart, O God, and renew a steadfast spirit within me.
Psalm 51:10

~

And if ye have not been faithful in that which is another man's, who shall give you that which is your own?
Luke 16:12 KJV

The young man who would succeed must identify his interests with those of his employer and exercise the same diligence in matters entrusted to him as he would in his own affairs.

It is the amount and excellence of what is over and above the required that determines the greatness of ultimate distinction.

Having confidence in your obedience, I write to you, knowing that you will do even more than I say.
Philemon 1:21
NKJV

53

Be a good workman, one who does not need to be ashamed when God examines your work. Know what his Word says and means.

2 Timothy 2:15 TLB

∼

To become an able and successful man in any profession, three things are necessary: nature, study, and practice.

54

If you wish success in life, make *perseverance* your bosom friend, *experience* your wise counselor, *caution* your elder brother, and *hope* your guardian genius.

Knowing that tribulation brings about perseverance; and perseverance, proven character; and proven character, hope; and hope does not disappoint.
Romans 5:3-5
NASB

The worst bankrupt in the world is the man who has lost his enthusiasm. Let a man lose everything else in the world but his enthusiasm and he will come through again to success.

It is fine to be zealous, provided the purpose is good, and to be so always.
Galatians 4:18

~

D o not attempt to do a thing unless you are sure of yourself; but do not relinquish it simply because someone else is not sure of you.

In quietness and confidence shall be your strength.
Isaiah 30:15 NKJV

As has been written, "Let the boaster boast in the Lord."
1 Corinthians 1:31 MLB

≈

The worst use that can be made of success is to boast of it.

Aim at perfection in every thing, though in most things it is unattainable; however, they who aim at it, and persevere, will come much nearer to it, than those whose laziness and despondency make them give it up as unattainable.

You are to be perfect, even as your Father in heaven is perfect.
Matthew 5:48 TLB

Under his direction the whole body is fitted together perfectly, and each part in its own special way helps the other parts, so that the whole body is healthy and growing and full of love.
Ephesians 4:16
TLB
~

Never one thing and seldom one person can make for a success. It takes a number of them merging into one perfect whole.

Snowflakes are one of nature's most fragile things, but just look what they can do when they stick together.

Let us not give up meeting together, as some are in the habit of doing, but let us encourage one another.
Hebrews 10:25

61

He lifted me out of the slimy pit, out of the mud and mire; he set my feet on a rock and gave me a firm place to stand.
Psalm 40:2

Behind every successful man there's a lot of unsuccessful years.

Success generally depends upon knowing how long it takes to succeed.

Perseverance must finish its work so that you may be mature and complete, not lacking anything.
James 1:4

If you want to build a tower, you first sit down and decide how much it will cost, to see if you have enough money to finish the job.
Luke 14:28 NCV

No man will succeed unless he is ready to face and overcome difficulties and prepared to assume responsibilities.

Many people have the ambition to succeed; they may even have special aptitude for their job. And yet they do not move ahead. Why? Perhaps they think that since they can master the job, there is no need to master themselves.

He that hath no rule over his own spirit is like a city that is broken down, and without walls.
Proverbs 25:28
KJV

65

Blessed is the man who listens to me, watching daily at my gates, waiting at my doorposts, for he who finds me finds life, and obtains favor from the Lord.
Proverbs 8:34-35
NASB

The recipe for successful achievement:

1. Enjoy your work.
2. Do your best.
3. Develop good working relationships.
4. Be open to opportunities.

A long time ago a noted specialist said that his secret of success as a physician was keeping the patient's head cool and his feet warm. And it is just now becoming generally known that a "hot head" and "cold feet" are enough to bring disaster to even a well man.

He who is slow to anger is better than the mighty. And he who rules his spirit than he who takes a city.
Proverbs 16:32
NKJV

I press toward the goal for the prize of the upward call of God in Christ Jesus.
Philippians 3:14
NKJV

❧

No wind blows in favor of a ship without a destination.

If you don't like the road you're walking, start paving another one.

Rise up; this matter is in your hands. We will support you, so take courage and do it.
Ezra 10:4

Even a fool is thought wise if he keeps silent, and discerning if he holds his tongue.
Proverbs 17:28

~

L ess is more is true not only in writing, but in life.

Success for the striver washes away the effort of striving.

They that sow in tears shall reap in joy.
Psalm 126:5 KJV

~

Therefore do not be foolish, but understand what the Lord's will is.
Ephesians 5:17

~

There is nothing like a fixed, steady aim, with an honorable purpose. It dignifies your nature, and insures your success.

If you have a good name...if you can face your God and say, "I have done my best," then you are a success.

A good name is rather to be chosen than great riches, and loving favour rather than silver and gold.
Proverbs 22:1 KJV

Put in the sickle for the harvest is ripe.
Joel 3:13 NASB

H e that would have fruit must climb the tree.

74

The gent who wakes up and finds himself a success hasn't been asleep.

Whatever your hand finds to do, do it with all your might.
Ecclesiastes 9:10

We are confident that we have a good conscience, in all things desiring to live honorably.
Hebrews 13:18
NKJV

The necessary ingredients for enjoying success:
1. Simple tastes
2. A certain degree of courage
3. Self-denial to a point
4. Love of work
5. A clear conscience

The most important single ingredient in the formula of success is knowing how to get along with people.

In humility consider others better than yourselves. Each of you should look not only to your own interests, but also to the interests of others.
Philippians 2:3-4

He knows enough to refuse evil and choose good.
Isaiah 7:15 NASB

～

Lasting success rarely comes to those who do not first decide to succeed.

We would accomplish many more things if we did not think of them as impossible.

The things impossible with men are possible with God.
Luke 18:27 NASB

Confess your faults one to another, and pray one for another, that ye may be healed.
James 5:16 KJV

~

I have made mistakes, but I have never made the mistake of claiming that I never made one.

Success is never final and failure never fatal. It's courage that counts.

So we say with confidence, "The Lord is my helper, I will not be afraid. What can man do to me?"
Hebrews 13:6

For he has delivered me from all my troubles, and my eyes have looked in triumph on my foes.
Psalms 54:7

Failure is the halfway mark on the road to success.

Failure is often that early morning hour of darkness which precedes the dawning of the day of success.

In the world ye shall have tribulation: but be of good cheer; I have overcome the world.
John 16:33 KJV

So David triumphed over the Philistine with a sling and a stone; without a sword in his hand he struck down the Philistine and killed him.
1 Samuel 17:50

∽

I couldn't wait for success ...so I went ahead without it.

84

Success requires the vision to see, the faith to believe, and the courage to do.

Be on your guard; stand firm in the faith; be men of courage; be strong.
1 Corinthians 16:13

~

*The gate is small
and the road is
narrow that leads
to true life.
Matthew 7:14
NCV*

There are no shortcuts to any place worth going.

86

Don't wait for your ship to come in; swim out to it.

I am the Lord, who opens a way through the waters, making a path right through the sea.
Isaiah 43:16 TLB

*But as for me,
I walk in
my integrity.
Psalm 26:11 NRSV*

Every man should make up his mind that if he expects to succeed, he must give an honest return for the other man's dollar.

Character is the real foundation of all worthwhile success.

Walk in the way of goodness, and keep to the paths of righteousness. For the upright will dwell in the land.
Proverbs 2:20-21
NKJV

Diligent hands will rule, but laziness ends in slave labor.
Proverbs 12:24

I t takes twenty years to make an overnight success.

To climb steep hills
Requires slow pace
at first.

*Though your
beginning was
small, yet your
latter end would
greatly increase.
Job 8:7 AMP*

So we make it our goal to please him.
2 Corinthians 5:9

Always aim for achievement and forget about success.

To follow, without halt, one aim: There's the secret of success.

But Jesus told him, "Anyone who lets himself be distracted from the work I plan for him is not fit for the Kingdom of God."
Luke 9:62 TLB

[Jesus] got up, rebuked the wind and said to the waves, "Quiet! Be still!" Then the wind died down and it was completely calm. He who believes in Me, the works that I do shall he do also.
Mark 4:39 NIV,
John 14:12 NASB
~

The world is not interested in the storms you encountered, but did you bring in the ship?

The measure of success is not whether you have a tough problem to deal with, but whether it's the same problem you had last year.

But the God of all grace, who hath called us unto his eternal glory by Christ Jesus, after that ye have suffered a while, make you perfect, stablish, strengthen, settle you.
1 Peter 5:10 KJV

My soul shall be joyful in the Lord; it shall rejoice in His salvation.
Psalm 35:9 NKJV

~

The strength of a man consists in finding out the way God is going, and going that way.

Four steps to achievement: plan purposefully, prepare prayerfully, proceed positively, pursue persistently.

Now all the work of Solomon was well-ordered from the day of the foundation of the house of the Lord until it was finished. So the house of the Lord was completed.
2 Chronicles 8:16
NKJV

But God hath chosen the foolish things of the world to confound the wise; and God hath chosen the weak things of the world to confound the things which are mighty.
1 Corinthians 1:27 KJV

~

The secret of all victory lies in the organization of the non-obvious.

Success in life comes not from holding a good hand, but in playing a poor hand well.

To him who overcomes, I will grant to eat of the tree of life.
Revelation 2:7
NASB

But remember the Lord your God, for it is he who gives you power to get wealth, so that he may confirm his covenant that he swore to your ancestors.
Deuteronomy 8:18 NRSV

The talent of success is nothing more than doing what you can do well; and doing well whatever you do, without a thought of fame.

A winner is someone who recognizes his God-given talents, works his tail off to develop them into skills, and uses these skills to accomplish his goals.

The man who had received the five talents brought the other five. "Master," he said, "you entrusted me with five talents. See, I have gained five more."
Matthew 25:20

"*My food*," *said Jesus, "is to do the will of him who sent me and to finish his work.*"
John 4:34

~

There is no limit to the good a man can do if he doesn't care who gets the credit.

There is no substitute for hard work.

He who cultivates his land will have plenty of bread, but he who follows worthless people and pursuits will have poverty enough.
Proverbs 28:19
AMP

Seek those things which are above.
Colossians 3:1
NKJV
~

If you succeed in all you do, it's a sure sign you're not reaching high enough.

Those who aim low usually hit their targets.

For as he thinketh in his heart, so is he.
Proverbs 23:7
KJV

Do you see a man skilled in his work? He will serve before kings; he will not serve before obscure men.
Proverbs 22:29

Do in life what you would do even if no one paid you for it — do what you are passionate about. Soon men will pay almost anything for your services.

The successful person is the individual who forms the habit of doing what the failing person doesn't like to do.

Go watch the ants, you lazy person. Watch what they do and be wise.
Proverbs 6:6 NCV

*If you do what
the Lord wants,
he will make
certain each step
you take is sure.
The Lord will
hold your hand,
and if you
stumble, you
still won't fall.*
Psalm 37:23-24
CEV

Y ou have to experience
   failure in order to
understand success.

A wise man will make more opportunity than he finds.

A man's gift maketh room for him, and bringeth him before great men.
Proverbs 18:16
KJV

Correct those with understanding, and they will gain knowledge.
Proverbs 19:25
NCV
~

A failure is a man who has blundered, but is not able to cash in on the experience.

More people talk themselves into failure than talk themselves into success.

Your words now reflect your fate then: either you will be justified by them or you will be condemned.
Matthew 12:37
TLB

~

Take delight in the Lord, and he will give you the desires of your heart.
Psalm 37:4 NRSV

~

Don't aim for success if you want it; just do what you love and believe in, and it will come naturally.

Happiness, wealth, and success are by-products...they should not be the goal.

Seek first His kingdom and His righteousness; and all these things shall be added to you.
Matthew 6:33
NASB

*Is anything
too difficult
for the Lord?
Genesis 18:14
NASB*

Determine that the thing can and shall be done, and then we shall find the way.

Confidence of success ...often induces real success.

Being confident of this very thing, that he which hath begun a good work in you will perform it until the day of Jesus Christ. Philippians 1:6 KJV

~

He who finds his life will lose it, and he who loses his life for My sake will find it.
Matthew 10:39
NKJV

Falling in love with one's job is the secret of success.

116

Success lies in this: Do your best. Then expect God's best.

All these blessings shall come upon you and overtake you, because you obey the voice of the Lord your God. Deuteronomy 28:2 NKJV

As the deer pants for the water brooks, so pants my soul for You, O God.
Psalm 42:1 NKJV

~

The only people who achieve much are those who want knowledge so badly that they seek it while the conditions are still unfavorable.

Yͭou have to want it [success] bad. You can find geniuses on any skid row and average intellects as presidents of banks. It's what pushes you from inside.

Do you not know that in a race all the runners run, but only one gets the prize? Run in such a way as to get the prize.
1 Corinthians 9:24

When Gideon came to the Jordan, he and the three hundred men who were with him crossed over, exhausted but still in pursuit.
Judges 8:4 NKJV
~

Let me tell you the secret that has led me to my goal. My strength lies solely in my tenacity.

On the clarity of your ideas depends the scope of your success in any endeavor.

So I turned my mind to understand, to investigate and to search out wisdom and the scheme of things and to understand the stupidity of wickedness and the madness of folly.
Ecclesiastes 7:25

We want each of you to show this same diligence to the very end, in order to make your hope sure.
Hebrews 6:11

The road to success is dotted with many tempting parking places.

122

Success results as much from what we don't choose to do as it does from what we choose to do.

I have set before you life or death, blessing or curse. Oh, that you would choose life.
Deuteronomy 30:19 TLB

123

Though a righteous man falls seven times, he rises again.
Proverbs 24:16

~

Success consists of getting up more times than you fall.

124

One of the most important lessons of life is that success must continually be won and is never finally achieved.

For everyone who keeps on asking receives; and he who keeps on seeking finds; and to him who keeps on knocking, [the door] will be opened.
Matthew 7:8 AMP

125

Hold on to what you have, so that no one will take your crown.
Revelation 3:11

~

You may have to fight a battle more than once to win it.

Diligence is the mother of good fortune.

The plans of the diligent lead surely to advantage, but everyone who is hasty comes surely to poverty.
Proverbs 21:5
NASB

127

*Keep a clear
conscience so that
those who speak
evil of your good
life in Christ
will be made
ashamed.*
1 Peter 3:16 NCV

Success in life depends
upon the three I's:
integrity, intelligence,
and industry.

Success is peace of mind, which is a direct result of knowing you did your best to become the best that you are capable of becoming.

Do not conform any longer to the pattern of this world, but be transformed by the renewing of your mind. Then you will be able to test and approve what God's will is — his good, pleasing and perfect will.
Romans 12:2

129

Better a patient man than a warrior, a man who controls his temper than one who takes a city.
Proverbs 16:32

The secret of success is to be like a duck — smooth and unruffled on the top, but paddling furiously underneath.

If A is success in life, then A equals x plus y plus z. Work is x, y is play, and z is keeping your mouth shut.

Those who are careful about what they say keep themselves out of trouble.
Proverbs 21:23
NCV

But they that wait upon the Lord shall renew their strength; they shall mount up with wings as eagles; they shall run, and not be weary; and they shall walk, and not faint.
Isaiah 40:31 KJV

A great secret of success is to go through life as a man who never gets used up.

Success is not the result of spontaneous combustion. You must set yourself on fire.

For this reason I remind you to fan into flame the gift of God.
2 Timothy 1:6

~

The wicked man does deceptive work, but he who sows righteousness will have a sure reward.
Proverbs 11:18
NKJV

The difference between failure and success is doing a thing nearly right and doing it exactly right.

Make yourself indispensable and you'll be moved up. Act as if you're indispensable and you'll be moved out.

Solomon, seeing that the young man was industrious, made him the officer over all the labor force of the house of Joseph.
1 Kings 11:28
NKJV

Blessed is the man who fears the Lord, who finds great delight in his commands. His children will be mighty in the land.
Psalm 112:1-2

∼

I have never believed that any success outside the home can compensate for failure within it.

If you want to learn about success, listen to someone who has succeeded.

Hear, O sons, the instruction of a father, and give attention that you may gain under-standing, for I give you sound teaching.
Proverbs 4:1-2
NASB

Suppose one of you wants to build a tower. Will he not first sit down and estimate the cost to see if he has enough money to complete it?
Luke 14:28

∼

Before everything else, getting ready is the secret of success.

138

Success is achieving the goals you have set for yourself.

But the noble man devises noble plans; and by noble plans he stands.
Isaiah 32:8 NASB

Am I now trying to win the approval of men, or of God? Or am I trying to please men? If I were still trying to please men, I would not be a servant of Christ.
Galatians 1:10

I cannot give you the formula for success but I can give you the formula for failure — which is: Try to please everybody.

There are no secrets to success. It is the result of preparation, hard work, learning from failure.

Sow for yourselves righteousness, reap the fruit of unfailing love, and break up your unplowed ground; for it is time to seek the Lord.
Hosea 10:12

All hard work brings a profit, but mere talk leads only to poverty.
Proverbs 14:23

~

It is always easy to covet another man's success without envying his labors.

Try not to become a man of success but rather try to become a man of value.

Turn my heart to your decrees, and not to selfish gain.
Psalm 119:36
NRSV

143

If you have faith as a mustard seed, you shall say to this mountain, "Move from here to there," and it shall move; and nothing shall be impossible to you.
Matthew 17:20
NASB

~

Small numbers make no difference to God. There is nothing small if God is in it.

144

It is not enough to begin; continuance is necessary. Success depends upon staying power.

Be steadfast, immovable, always abounding in the work of the Lord, knowing that your labor is not in vain in the Lord.
1 Corinthians 15:58 NKJV

Each of you should look not only to your own interests, but also to the interests of others.
Philippians 2:4

~

It is a deep-seated belief on the part of almost all Americans that their success will be better assured as they help to build the success of others.

Success is to be measured not by wealth, power, or fame, but by the ratio between what a man is and what he might be.

The Lord judges the peoples; judge me, O Lord, according to my righteousness and according to the integrity that is in me.
Psalm 7:8 NRSV

Happy is he...
whose hope is in
the Lord his God.
Psalm 146:5
NKJV

The bridge between failure and success is hope.

How you *define* success determines to a great extent whether you succeed.

Then Job answered the Lord, and said, I know that thou canst do every thing... So the Lord blessed the latter end of Job more than his beginning.
Job 42:1,2,12 KJV

149

Desire that ye might be filled with the knowledge of his will in all wisdom and spiritual understanding; That ye might walk worthy of the Lord unto all pleasing, being fruitful in every good work.
Colossians 1:9-10
KJV

To find his place and fill it is success for a man.

He has achieved success who has lived well, laughed often, and loved much.

I know the best thing we can do is to always enjoy life.
Ecclesiastes 3:12
CEV

Bear ye one another's burdens, and so fulfill the law of Christ.
Galatians 6:2 KJV

~

And I can live my life on earth
Contented to the end,
If but a few shall
know my worth
And proudly call me friend.

Wealth to us is not mere material for vainglory but an opportunity for achievement.

From everyone who has been given much shall much be required; and to whom they entrusted much, of him they will ask all the more.
Luke 12:48 NASB

153

Grace and peace be multiplied unto you through the knowledge of God, and of Jesus our Lord, According as his divine power hath given unto us all things that pertain unto life and godliness, through the knowledge of him that hath called us to glory and virtue.
2 Peter 1:2-3

Success is...seeking, knowing, loving and obeying God. If you seek, you will know; if you know, you will love; if you love, you will obey.

References

Acknowledgments

Charles Colson (6), Booker T. Washington (7), Baron Pierre de Coubertin (8), Thomas Jefferson (9), Helen Keller (10), Grantland Rice (12), English Proverb (13), Charles Buxton (14), Logan Pearsall Smith (15), Vince Lombardi (16), Thomas Carlyle (17), Corrie ten Boom (19), H. M. Field (20), Norman Vincent Peale (21), Chapin (23), C. W. Wendte (24), Ron Dentinger (25), Harry J. Kaiser (26), Herschel Walker (27), Loretta Lynn (28), Huey P. Long (29), T. T. Munger (31), George Washington Carver (32), W. E. B. Du Bois (33), Carl Sandburg (35), Ben Azzai (36), An Wang (37), Bear Bryant (38), B. C. Forbes (39), Arthur Ashe (40), William Menninger (41), Henry P. Davison (42), Wofford B. Camp (43), Joseph French Johnson (44), Henry Ford (45,138), John Greenleaf Whittier (46), Homer (47), Charles "Tremendous" Jones (48,85), Dr. Frank Crane (49), Richard Brinsley Sheridan (50), Sammy Kershaw (51), A. T. Mercie (52), Charles Kendall Adams (53), Henry Ward Beecher (54,72,96), Joseph Addison (55), H. W. Arnold (56), Stewart E. White (57), Arthur Helps (58), Philip Chesterfield (59), Marie Dressler (60), Vesta M. Kelly (61), Bob Brown (62), Charles-Lewis de Secondat, Baron de Montesquieu (63), William J. H. Boetcker (64), John Stevenson (65), Denis Waitley and Reni Witt (66), O. Byron Cooper (67), Dolly Pardon (69) Pendar (71), Ann Landers (73), Thomas Fuller (74), Wilson Mizner (75), George Sand (76),

Theodore Roosevelt (77), C. Malesherbez (79), James Gordon Bennett (80), George F. Tilton (81), A. L. Williams (82), Leigh Mitchell Hodges (83), Jonathan Winters (84), Beverly Sills (86), E. H. Harriman (88), John Hayes Hammond (89), Eddie Cantor (90), William Shakespeare (91), Helen Hayes (92), Anna Pavlova (93), William A. Ward (97), Oswald Spengler (98), Henry Wadsworth Longfellow (100), Larry Bird (101), Joseph Heller (103), Marvin Feldman (104), Donald Riggs (107), Jackie Sherrill (108), Fancis Bacon (109), Albert Hubbard (110), David Frost (112), Abraham Lincoln (114), Sigmund Freud (115), Oral Roberts (117), C. S. Lewis (118), Charley Winner (119), Louis Pasteur (120), James Robertson (121), Oliver Goldsmith (124), Charles Evans Hughes (125), Margaret Thatcher (126), Miguel de Cervantes (127), Charles Rupert Stockard (128), John Wooden (129), Albert Einstein (131,143), Albert Schweitzer (132), Reggie Leach (133), Edward D. Simmons (134), David Gardner (136), Edward I. Koch (139), Herbert Bayard Swope (140), Colin L. Powell (141), D. L. Moody (144), J. R. Miller (145), Paul G. Hoffman (146), H. G. Wells (147), Phillips Brooks (150), Bessie A. Stanley (151), Edgar A. Guest (152), Thucydides (153), Charles Malik (154).

Dear Reader:

If you would like to share with us a couple of your favorite quotes or ideas on the subject of success, we'd love to hear from you. Our address is:

Honor Books
P.O. Box 55388, Dept. J.
Tulsa, Oklahoma 74155

Additional Copies of this book and other titles in the
God's Little Instruction Book series are available at your local bookstore.

God's Little Instruction Book
God's Little Instruction Book II
God's Little Instruction Book for Mom
God's Little Instruction Book for Dad
God's Little Instruction Book for Graduates
God's Little Instruction Book for Students
God's Little Instruction Book for Kids
God's Little Instruction Book for Couples
God's Little Instruction Book for Men
God's Little Instruction Book — Special Gift Edition
God's Little Instruction Book Daily Calendar
God's Little Instruction Book for Women

Tulsa, Oklahoma